CHOPIN

AN INTRODUCTION TO HIS PIANO WORKS

EDITED BY WILLARD A. PALMER

Portrait by Marie Wodzińska (c. 1835)
(Musée Carnavalet, Paris)

CONTENTS

Second Edition

Copyright © MCMXCII by Alfred Publishing Co., Inc.

Cover art: A portrait of Chopin
by Eugène Delacroix (French, 1798–1863)
Louvre, Paris
Giraudon / Art Resource, New York

 A CD recording entitled *Falling in Love with Chopin*, which contains the selections in *Chopin—An Introduction to His Piano Works* performed by Valery Lloyd-Watts, is available separately (#4013).

Photographed in 1849

FREDERIC CHOPIN

Frederic Francois Chopin was born at Zelazowa Wola, a small village near Warsaw, Poland, on February 22, 1810. His father was a professor of French at the Lyceum of Warsaw and was employed as a private tutor to the children of Countess Louise Skarbek. Chopin's mother was the personal attendant of the Countess. The relationship between the Chopin family and the Skarbek family was a close one, and this proved to be a valuable asset to Frederic, since the Skarbeks actually owned the village of Zelazowa Wola. Frederic was the third child in the family, and from the day of his birth he heard music played on the piano by his sister, Louise, and his mother. As soon as Chopin was old enough to realize that he, too, could learn to make music at the piano he insisted that his sister teach him. So Louise, not yet ten years of age, became his first instructor. When his father decided that Louise should be allowed to study music with Adalbert Żywny, Frederic begged to be allowed to take lessons also. His request was granted in 1816, when he was only six years old.

Many believed Chopin's natural gifts rivaled those of Mozart. The *Polonaise in B♭ Major* (see page 23) is an example of his ability to compose at the age of seven. In the same year of his childhood, his *Polonaise in G Minor*, dedicated to the Countess Victoire Skarbek, was published (see page 39). It was hailed by many as a work of genius.

Frederic, known to his friends as Frycek (Fritsek), was a delicate child, but not a sickly one. His interests were many. He wrote poetry of some merit, showed considerable talent in drawing, was an excellent mimic, had a keen sense of humor, and his childhood was by no means a dull one.

By the time he was 12, Frycek had outgrown his teacher musically, but Żywny had given him a thorough grounding in the works of masters such as Mozart, Haydn and Beethoven, and especially the keyboard music of J.S. Bach, to whom Żywny was particularly devoted.

In 1822, Chopin's parents placed him under the guidance of Joseph Elsner, who was head of the conservatory at Warsaw, with whom he studied composition. He formally entered the conservatory at the age of 16 and graduated in three years. Elsner's report reads: "Lessons in musical composition: Chopin, Frederic, third year student, amazing capabilities, a musical genius."

When Chopin appeared in Paris and Vienna, he found that the public had been conditioned to react principally to showmanship, dazzling feats of virtuosity, loud playing, and the more shallow elements of musical performance. Chopin's artistic nature rebelled against this. He was impressed, of course, with the technical achievements of the famous piano virtuoso, Franz Liszt, and with the incredible virtuosity of the legendary violinist, Niccolò Paganini, and their prowess undoubtedly inspired him to practice even more diligently; but he was already a virtuoso of the first rank. His own playing greatly impressed Liszt. Mendelssohn praised him highly. Schumann said, "Hats off! A genius!" Because of his limited strength, Chopin preferred to give his recitals in intimate salons rather than in concert halls. He made comparatively few public appearances during his lifetime. He received very high fees for piano lessons and was much in demand as a teacher. He was also very well paid for his compositions.

During his lifetime, Chopin composed over 200 piano compositions, most of which are still part of the active repertoire of concert pianists the world over. Even during his lifetime, the immense popularity of some of his *Mazurkas*,

Waltzes, *Nocturnes* and *Polonaises* brought him great fame, and few musicales were complete without the performance of several of these. His *Etudes* had a great share in the revelation of the possibilities of the piano. They were performed, along with the *Scherzos*, the *Ballades*, and his works for piano and orchestra, by Franz Liszt and other great concert artists of the time. But none of Chopin's works bears the stamp of genius more strongly than some of his smaller compositions; for example, the *Preludes*.

Although Chopin did not in his lifetime enjoy fame equal to that of Mendelssohn, Schumann, Liszt, Kalkbrenner or Hummel, today his works are performed more frequently than those of any of his contemporaries. He was the greatest of the romanticists (although he detested the word) and the first modernist. His innovations in pedaling and fingering, along with his introduction of new elements of style in playing, were to raise the art of pianism to a new pinnacle.

All of Chopin's works were completed in a life-span of only 39 years. He died October 17, 1849.

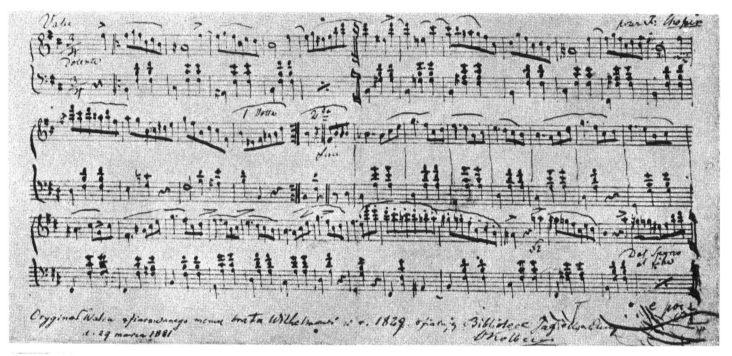

MANUSCRIPT COPY OF *WALTZ IN B MINOR Opus 69, No. 2* (beginning) from the collection of the Jagiellonian Library in Cracow. The inscription at the bottom of this manuscript is translated as follows:
The original manuscript of the Waltz, given to my brother Wilhelm in 1829,
I present to the Jagiellonian Library, March 29, 1881.
While this is not an autograph copy, it is the only known manuscript copy seemingly handed down from Chopin, who was a friend of the Kolberg family, one of whom studied with Chopin's teacher, Joseph Elsner. There is a more difficult version of this waltz, first published after Chopin's death by his friend, Jules Fontana. It is not necessarily a more authentic one than the version above, which is included in this INTRODUCTION because of its simplicity. The Fontana version may be found in Willard A. Palmer's edition of the Complete Waltzes of Chopin.

CHOPIN'S STYLE

How often we hear the music of Chopin performed in the so-called "grand manner," with excesses of sentimentality, exaggerated rubatos, and flashy virtuosity! That this is precisely the kind of playing Chopin abhorred is verified in numerous documented accounts by musicians who knew him, heard him play, and to whom he expressed his opinions. One of his students, Friederike Müller, who became a concert pianist of high reputation, kept a remarkably detailed record of her lessons with Chopin. The following excerpt from her diary is very informative:

His playing was always noble and beautiful; his tones sang, whether in full forte or softest piano. He took infinite pains to teach his pupils this legato, cantible style of playing. His most severe criticism was "He—— or she— does not know how to join two notes together." He also demanded the strictest adherence to rhythm. He hated all lingering and dragging, misplaced rubatos, as well as exaggerated ritardandos . . . . . and it is precisely in this respect that people make such terrible errors in playing his works.

Many glowing reports of Chopin's performances stress the beauty of his tone and the ease with which he played. It was a critic of *France Musicale* who wrote:

> While listening to these tones, all these delicate shadings that follow one after another intermingle, diverge, and reunite toward one and the same goal—melody—can you not believe you hear tiny voices whispering under silver bells, or a shower of pearls on crystal tables? The pianist's fingers seem to multiply *ad infinitum*. It seems impossible that two hands can create such effects of swiftness so calmly and naturally.

Chopin emphasized the importance of developing such control. When Mlle. Müller heard Franz Liszt play, Chopin asked her what impressed her most. She replied that it was his "calmness in overcoming the greatest technical difficulties." To this, Chopin answered:

> Simplicity is the final achievement. After one has conquered all the difficulties, after one has played a vast quantity of notes and more notes, it is simplicity that emerges in all its charm as the ultimate crowning reward of art.

Less than a year before he died, Chopin played several very successful concerts in London. The following excerpt from the *London Daily News*, July 10th, 1848, tells of how well Chopin had achieved this reward:

> He accomplishes enormous difficulties, but so quietly, so smoothly and with such constant delicacy and refinement that the listener is not sensible of their real magnitude.

Although it is known that Chopin was physically incapable of achieving the powerful effects demanded by many of his works, one must never conclude that dynamic contrasts were unimportant to him. Of this Moscheles wrote, "His soft playing being a mere breath, he needs no powerful forte to produce the desired contrasts." It is evident that Chopin employed "super-pianissimos" with great effect. In his music we often find the words *sotto voce* and *mezzo voce*, words closely linking the music with the cantabile style he so often demanded, at the same time calling for a particular kind of controlled softness and tonal quality. But this does not mean that Chopin's music should be scaled downward in volume. Those who may believe that a delicate murmur was all he ever drew from his instrument may be startled to read an account by George Mathis, his pupil and friend:

> Those who heard Chopin play may say that nothing approaching it has ever been heard. What virtuosity! What power! Yes, what power! But it only lasted a few bars; and what exaltation and inspiration! The man's whole being vibrated. The piano was animated by the intensest life: it sent a thrill through you!

And Carl Mikuli, who studied with him in Paris, wrote:

> The tone Chopin drew from the instrument, especially in cantabile passages, was immense . . . . a manly energy gave to appropriate passages an overpowering effect of energy without coarseness. But, on the other hand, he knew how to enchant the listener with delicacy, without affectation.

Chopin made it very clear that he would never wish to impose his own physical limitations upon his music in the hands of other performers. On one occasion a young man played the *Polonaise Militaire* for Chopin with such vigor that he broke a string. He apologized profusely. Chopin was not disturbed. "Young man," he said, "if I had your strength and could play that polonaise as it should be played, there would be no strings left on the instrument when I finished!" It seems clear that when Chopin indicated a fortissimo, he meant it.

What Chopin disliked most was the over-dramatization of any music. Although he admired Franz Liszt, he could not tolerate that element in his playing. Once while he was listening as Liszt played a Beethoven sonata he remarked, "Must he play everything in such a declamatory manner?"

MORE ABOUT *Tempo Rubato*

Perhaps the most abused effect used in the playing of Chopin's music is the *tempo rubato*. The word means, of course, "stolen time," and it must be remembered that time taken from one part of a measure must be added to another part. In explaining rubato to his pupil, Wilhelm von Lenz, Chopin said, "The left hand is the conductor. It must never waver or lose ground, no matter what is done with the right hand." Chopin's first biographer, Moritz Karakowski, described his rubato by saying, "The bass went along in quite regular time, while the right hand moved in complete freedom." Can Chopin's rubato then be far removed from Mozart's? In October of 1777, Mozart wrote to his father:

Everyone is surprised that I always remain strictly in time; they cannot understand that the left hand should not in the least be concerned in *tempo rubato*. When they play, the left hand always follows along.

Franz Liszt and Chopin's pupil, Carl Mikuli, both testified that in playing rubato Chopin never varied the basic meter. It should be very clear from such evidence that Chopin would not have approved of the lavishly free rubatos so often employed in the performance of his music. When the underlying pulse of the music is distorted, Chopin's music is not being played as the composer intended. It is important to observe that *no note-value should ever be so increased or decreased that it could have been more accurately written as a note of a different value.* Chopin certainly wrote what he wanted to hear as precisely as musical notation would allow.

CHOPIN'S ORNAMENTATION

Research revealing valid information concerning the correct performance of Chopin's ornaments is long overdue. Since the latter part of the 19th century, Chopin's music has been performed in the traditions of Hummel, Czerny, Liszt, and Leschetitzky. But the breaking of the old tradition began with Hummel and his followers, not with Chopin.

The rules for the performance of ornaments prescribed by J.S. Bach, C.P.E. Bach, Leopold Mozart, Johann J. Quantz, Francois Couperin and scores of other famed musicians of the 18th century survived throughout the Classical period. They were not simply dismissed during the Romantic period. These rules were endorsed by all the great masters, including Beethoven, Haydn, Mozart and Clementi; it was in the traditions of these masters that Chopin was educated. Because his style was formed in his early years in Poland, he was relatively isolated from European Romanticists. His earliest compositions reflect his schooling in the old traditions but also show the beginnings of his later and more mature style.

It was Hummel who made the widely-accepted decision that so profoundly affected the performance of ornaments, particularly the trill. In his famous and successful method book, published around 1828, he stated that "in general every trill should begin on the note itself, and not on the auxiliary note above." Hummel's reasoning was elementary:

1. It is generally more convenient to begin on the main note.

2. Beginning on the upper note tends to obscure the melody note, which ought to be more strongly impressed on the ear.

These reasons might seem logical even now, if we were not so aware of the harmonic function of the traditional baroque and classical trill, which is to produce momentary dissonance that adds tension and excitement to the melody, and which can often remove from the most banal tunes some of their superficiality.

But Chopin's ornaments were *functional*, not merely decorative. Hummel, Czerny, Liszt and others used ornaments to supply pretty "curlicues," but to Chopin such use of respected devices would have been repulsive. Carl Mikuli, who studied with Chopin, and whose edition of Chopin's works was the standard for many years, wrote the following in the foreword to his edition:

In the trill, *which he generally commenced on the auxiliary*, he required perfect evenness rather than great rapidity, the closing turn to be played easily and without haste. (Italics by the editor of the present edition.)

After making such a statement, Mikuli made his edition without observing this rule at all! But one must bear in mind that Mikuli was Chopin's student for less than a year, and during that same year he was studying with other teachers. Like most of the pianists of the Romantic period he was caught up in the schools of Hummel, Czerny and Liszt. He was no musicologist, and is known even to have confused Chopin's autographs with those of a copyist. His edition, containing so many emendations said to have had Chopin's personal endorsement, was published many years after Chopin's death, when every concert pianist had succumbed to the practices recommended by Hummel. While Mikuli's edition is valuable and contains much that is important, it cannot be unconditionally accepted as reflecting all of Chopin's intentions.

An exact parallel may be drawn in the case of Carl Czerny, who studied several years with Beethoven. Beethoven accepted him as a pupil on the condition that he study C.P.E. Bach's rules for playing ornaments. In spite of this, Czerny flagrantly violated these rules in his editions of the music of J.S. Bach and Beethoven! Czerny studied much more with Hummel than he did with Beethoven. Hummel also taught Henselt and Thalberg. Czerny taught Liszt and Leschetitzky, each of whom taught hundreds of prominent artists and influenced thousands more. To these disciples of Hummel the new rules were retroactive and were applied to the music of every period, regardless of the composers' intentions. In the hands of these musicians, regardless of their excellence in other respects, the ornaments of all composers were played alike, and the present misconception of the intentions of many composers was formed and perpetuated.

By the beginning of the 20th century it had become fashionable to play all the "grace notes" (appoggiaturas) AHEAD of the beat, even though this practice was forbidden in every respectable method book, including Hummel's! The long appoggiatura was all but forgotten, and no one played trills beginning on the upper note, even in the music of Bach.

Although many pianists will be startled at the idea of applying Bach's and Clementi's rules to the playing of Chopin, they may examine the evidence for themselves. They must consider the fact that Chopin used Clementi's method books with his own students. At the very beginning Clementi carefully discusses his rules for ornamentation and he applies these rules throughout his method. They must also consider that Chopin was thoroughly grounded in the teachings of C.P.E. Bach, and that he had J.S. Bach's *Well-Tempered Clavier* on his desk in Majorca when he wrote many of his *Preludes*.

With such facts in mind, Chopin's ornaments may be given more careful study than they have received. One must carefully consider the musical function of each ornament in the light of the musical traditions upon which Chopin's style was formed.

1. THE TRILL   ∿   *tr*

According to the tables of ornaments left by J.S. Bach (in the *Clavier-Büchlein vor Wilhelm Friedemann Bach*) and by C.P.E. Bach (in his *Essay on the True Art of Playing Keyboard Instruments*), the symbols ∿ and *tr* are synonymous. Both indicate trills, and all trills begin on the *upper* note. Mozart's father, Leopold, gives similar instructions in his method book for the violin. Muzio Clementi

also advocated beginning the trill on the upper note, but he made a few notable exceptions. The following excerpts from his famous method book, *Introduction to the Art of Playing on the Pianoforte*, show that the trill could begin on the principal note when it was to be played legato with the preceding note, or when the trill was used on transient or passing tones:

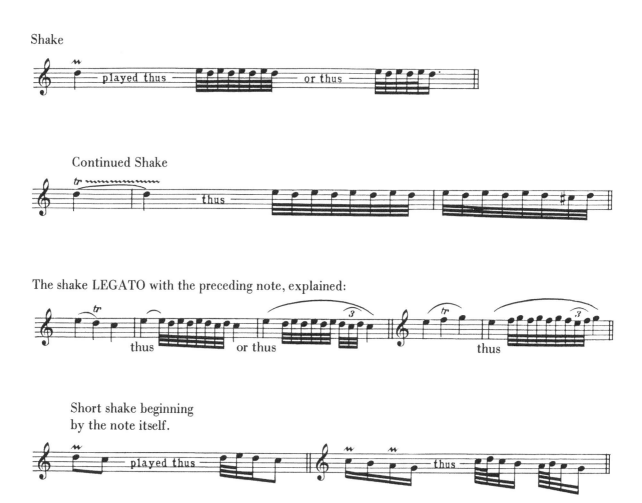

Shake

Continued Shake

The shake LEGATO with the preceding note, explained:

Short shake beginning
by the note itself.

Of trills, Clementi says, "The GENERAL mark for the shake is this *tr* and composers trust CHIEFLY to the taste and judgement of the performer, whether it shall be long, short, transient, or turned." (*Punctuation and capital letters are Clementi's.*)

In the above examples it will be noted that Clementi added a suffix (closing turn) at the end of the longer trills. Chopin usually indicated such a suffix with small notes, as will be

seen in examples that follow.

The importance of these rules is emphasized by the fact that they are taken from a method book which Chopin used with all his beginning students!

For important evidence that Chopin's early training led him to take the trill beginning on the upper note for granted, let us examine the following measures from the

Polonaise in A♭ Major, written when Chopin was only 11 (see page 56):

The realizations of the above trills, in lighter print, are supplied by the editor of the present edition. The musical function of these trills is obvious. The trills begin on the upper note, as the rules of Bach and Clementi dictate. The three-note motive beginning with the opening two sixteenth notes is developed by the trills, in augmentation. The motive is repeated in the slurred groups of notes following the second trill. Certainly the whole idea is utterly destroyed if the trills begin, as most modern editions show, on the principal note!

Additional evidence that Chopin regarded the trill as normally beginning on the upper note is found in his manner of indicating the prefixed trill. In the following example, the two small notes are played on the beat, and they lead into the trill beginning on the upper note:

Chopin, Opus 32, No. 2 (not included in this book)
written:

played:

or with additional repercussions of C-B♭.

Robert Schumann, on the other hand, regarded the trill as normally beginning on the principal note. He writes the prefixed trill accordingly. In the following example, the three small notes begin on the beat, and lead into the trill beginning on the principal note:

Schumann, Opus 3, No. 3
written:

The resulting manner of performance is identical to that of the Chopin example.

The fact that ⁓ and *tr* are synonymous has escaped most modern editors of Chopin's works. More than one editor has admitted his confusion in remarks to the effect that, for some inexplicable reason, Chopin has used ⁓ in one place and *tr* in another, when the notes of both passages are identical. It must be emphasized that either of these signs in Chopin's music can indicate a long trill, short trill, or transient trill (sometimes erroneously called an "upper mordent"). The manner of performance is determined by the character and style of the passage and often by the note preceding the ornament.

As additional proof that Chopin considered the symbols ⁓ and *tr* to mean one and the same thing, the following measures from the *Nocturne in E♭ Major*, Opus 9, No. 2 (not included in this book) are cited. Many similar instances can be found in other works of Chopin.

Measure 13
WRITTEN:

Measure 21
WRITTEN:

BOTH ARE
PLAYED:

Since this is an example of a trainsent or passing trill, it begins on the principal note, as Clementi indicated in his table.

In the present edition, ONE correct way of performing each trill is shown in light print on a small staff above the ornament. This is done in every case when the method of playing is not made perfectly obvious by a similar situation in a previous measure. It is important to remember that there are usually SEVERAL correct ways of playing any ornament. The realization will show the basic idea, and it may be varied to suit the taste and skill of the individual. Almost any trill may be played with more repercussions than the realization shows, if the performer has the skill and the desire to do so.

In the *Mazurka in B♭ Major* (Opus 7, No. 1) on page 42, measure 3 is written as follows:

The realization in light print indicates that the measure may be played as follows:

But it might also be played one of the following ways:

Some performers consider it more artistic to stop the trill on the principal note, to emphasize the melody. Some prefer to continue the trill right into the following note, as shown in the last example.

Situations exist, of course, in which it is difficult to determine whether the trill is best begun on the upper auxiliary or the principal note. In such cases, the decision is left, as Clementi says, to the taste and judgement of the performer.

2. THE APPOGGIATURA

Almost all appoggiaturas in Chopin's music are played *on the beat*, and the time values given the small notes are subtracted from the large note that immediately follows.

This is in accordance with the instructions of J.S. Bach, C.P.E. Bach, Leopold Mozart and Muzio Clementi.

Chopin used two types of single appoggiaturas:

a. The *long appoggiatura*, without a cross-stroke:

b. The *short appoggiatura*, with a cross stroke:

The latter sign was derived from an old method of writing sixteenth notes.

In accordance with the rules of the composers mentioned above, the long appoggiatura receives half the time of the principal note, except when the principal note is a dotted note. It then usually takes two-thirds of the value of the note. Chopin rarely used a long appoggiatura before a dotted note.

Long appoggiaturas are found in several of the pieces in this book. An example is found in the *Polonaise in B♭ Major* (Posthumous) (p. 23) in the 12th measure:

WRITTEN:

PLAYED:

The long appoggiatura generally received special emphasis, as the accent in the above realization indicates.

Short appoggiaturas are plentiful in Chopin's music. Before very quick notes they may still receive only half the value of the note, but they are generally played as rapidly as possible. The following example is from the *Mazurka in B♭ Major* (Opus 7, No. 1) (p. 42) in the 4th measure:

WRITTEN:

PLAYED:

or:

Exceptions to the rule that small notes are played on the beat occur in the following two instances:

a. When the small notes form the termination of a trill, as they do in the *Polonaise in A^b Major* (Posthumous) (p. 56) in the 5th measure:

WRITTEN: PLAYED:

b. When a small note appears immediately before a bar line, as it does in the *Mazurka in A Minor* (Opus 7, No. 2) (not included in this book):

WRITTEN: PLAYED:

A similar example occurs in the 25th measure of the *Mazurka in C Major* (Opus 67, No. 3) on page 21.

3. THE TURN

In Chopin's music the turn is used as follows:

a. Directly over the note
In this case, the turn begins on the note above the principal note. An example is found in the *Polonaise in B^b Major* (Posthumous) (p. 24), in the 13th measure:

WRITTEN: PLAYED:

b. After the note
In this case the turn is played after the principal note. An example is found in the *Prelude in E Minor* (Op. 28, No. 4) (p. 31) in the 16th measure:

WRITTEN: PLAYED: or:

When a turn is written out in small notes, rather than indicated by the symbol , it is played before the beat. An unusual example occurs in the *Waltz in A^b Major* (Opus 69, No. 1) (p. 48), in the 7th measure. In this example the small notes indicating the turn are followed by a normal short appoggiatura. The turn is played before the beat, but the short appoggiatura must be played on the beat:

WRITTEN: PLAYED: or:

12

4. THE ARPEGGIO

When one of the above symbols appears beside a chord, the chord is to be broken, beginning with the lowest note. If the symbol extends through both staffs, the chord is broken continuously from the lowest note of the lower staff to the highest note of the upper staff. If each hand has a separate sign, one above the other, the two hands may begin simultaneously, or the right hand may begin immedi-

ately after the first note of the left hand is played. In such cases the arpeggio begins *on the beat*.

When only the right hand has an arpeggio, it generally begins on the beat. In some cases a left hand arpeggio may anticipate the beat, so the last note occurs on the beat coinciding with the corresponding right hand note.

CHOPIN'S PEDALING

Chopin made great contributions to the art of pedaling, and his pedal markings should never be ignored. It is well to remember, however, that the pianos used by Chopin lacked the resonance of the modern piano, and that Chopin preferred uprights to grands. This accounts for many of the indications for long sustained pedaling that sometimes seem inappropriate on the modern piano. In all such cases, Chopin's pedaling should be tried and carefully considered before any slight alterations are made.

Chopin used the symbols *ped* ⊕ to show the application and release of the pedal. These markings are not as precise as the 20th-century symbol ⌐_____⌐; and with them it is not as easy to show when the pedal is to be released and depressed on the same note (⌐_____∧_____⌐). For this reason the present edition has adopted the more recently developed system.

It is true that Chopin's scores seldom indicate "overlapped" pedaling. Most often he uses *ped* ⊕ *ped* ⊕; which is known as "rhythmic" pedaling. The indications *ped ped* , used by Liszt so often, seem never to occur in Chopin's manuscripts, but sometimes the sign indicating the release of the pedal was writ-

ten almost directly over the sign indicating the depression of the pedal for the next group of notes. In other cases, the signs are written extremely close together. In these situations the use of the indication for overlapped pedaling (⌐_____∧_____⌐) seems completely appropriate.

In some of Chopin's autographs the pedaling is so meticulously indicated that there is absolutely no doubt about what he intended. In other cases the manuscripts show no pedaling at all, and the first editions were published with none. This is particularly true of many of the waltzes and mazurkas. Fortunately Chopin left enough examples of how he pedaled similar measures in other waltzes and mazurkas to give us a good idea of what to do in such cases. Sometimes Chopin omitted pedal marks in passages obviously pedaled the same as those in preceding measures. These omissions are especially frequent when an entire phrase occurring earlier in the composition is repeated. In this edition we have supplemented Chopin's pedal markings, but we have indicated all editorial additions by using light print for entire pedal marks, and dotted lines for releases within pedal marks that are so long that their effectiveness on the modern piano may be questionable.

METRONOME MARKINGS

Chopin occasionally gave his own metronome settings. When this is the case, they are given in this edition in dark print. Indications in light print are derived from early editions or supplied by the editor of the present edition.

Metronome markings in Chopin's music are in most cases of limited value, usually serving only to give an approximate idea of the tempo of the first few measures of the

main theme of the composition.

The question of tempo is not easily resolved. It depends not only on the factors of personal taste and skill, but to some extent upon the individual instrument and the room or hall involved in the performance. It is well to remember that Chopin detested velocity for the sake of showmanship, and that he also hated "all lingering and dragging."

RECOMMENDED READING

Bach, Carl Philipp Emanuel. ESSAY ON THE TRUE ART OF PLAYING KEYBOARD INSTRUMENTS, W.W. Norton & Co., New York, 1949.

Dorian, Frederick. THE HISTORY OF MUSIC IN PER-FORMANCE, W.W. Norton & Co., New York, 1942.

Hedley, Arthur. CHOPIN, J.M. Dent & Sons, Ltd., London, 1947. Paperback edition published by Collier Books, 1962.
> An important contribution to Chopin literature. Contains a wealth of information, much of it unearthed through the author's own scholarly research.

Niecks, Frederick. FREDERICK CHOPIN AS A MAN AND MUSICIAN, 2 vols. Novello, Ewer & Co., London and New York, 1888.
> A great work of nineteenth-century scholarship, containing much valuable information and a great deal of data that has subsequently been proven incorrect.

Schonberg, Harold C. THE GREAT PIANISTS FROM MOZART TO THE PRESENT, Simon and Schuster, New York, 1963.
> A delightful, engrossing and informative book that should be read by every pianist.

Walker, Alan. CHOPIN: PROFILES OF THE MAN AND THE MUSICIAN, Barrie & Rockliff, London 1966.
> A scholarly handbook. Contains essays by Badura-Skoda, L. Berkeley, R. Collet, P. Gould, P. Hamburger, A. Hedley, A. Hutchins, B. Jacobson, A. Rawsthorne, H. Searle, A. Walker.

Weinstock, Herbert. CHOPIN: THE MAN AND HIS MUSIC, Alfred Knopf, New York, 1949.
> A brilliant work of unquestionable integrity and scholarship. Easy to read and filled with valuable information.

ACKNOWLEDGEMENTS

I would like to express my sincere appreciation to Judith Simon Linder for her valued assistance in the preparation of the manuscript, and to Dorothy Veinus Hagan for translations from the French. I especially wish to thank Iris and Morton Manus for the meticulous care with which they helped me to prepare this edition.

WALTZ IN A MINOR

Posthumous

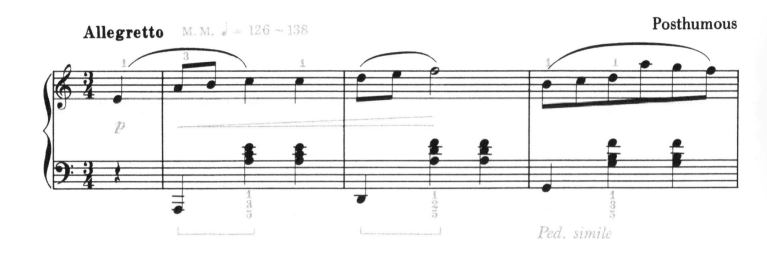

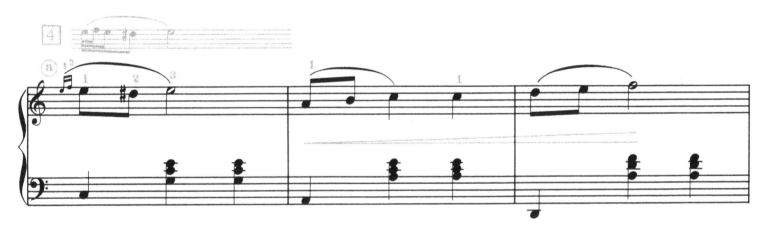

This waltz was not published until 1955, when it appeared in the French journal, *La Revue Musicale*, together with facsimiles of two autographs, which are preserved in the library of the Paris Conservatoire. It is here published for the first time in the U.S.

ⓐ All the appoggiaturas should be played quickly and *on the beat*.

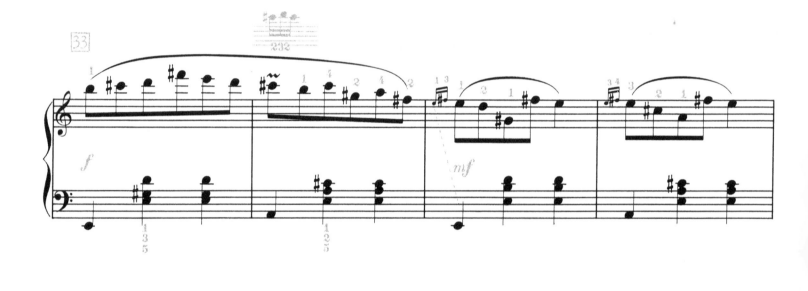

b The trill may have more repercussions:

18

ALBUMLEAF
to Emile Gaillard

Posthumous

The autograph of this selection is in the library of the Paris Conservatoire. It is signed, "F.F. Chopin, Paris, 20 July 1840." It was discovered in 1941 by Dr. Jacques Chailley, then secretary general of the Conservatoire, who brought it to the attention of the First International Musicological Congress Devoted to the Works of Frederic Chopin (Warsaw, 1960). The piece was found in an album belonging to Emile Gaillard, a friend and pupil of Chopin. Because the composer gave no title to the selection, Dr. Chailley suggested the title used above.

(a) All appoggiaturas in this selection should be played rapidly and *on the beat*.

Fine

mf – p

1.

2.

D. C. al Fine

MAZURKA IN C MAJOR
pour M-e. Hoffman

Allegretto M.M. ♩ = 144

Op. 67, No. 3
Posthumous

This is one of Chopin's shortest mazurkas. It is complete on these two pages. It was first published by A.M. Schlesinger in Berlin in 1855 in an edition by Jules Fontana. Fontana gives the date of composition as 1835.

(a) Throughout this composition Chopin uses the symbol *tr* to indicate short trills, most of which are *transient trills*. See pages 7 and 9.

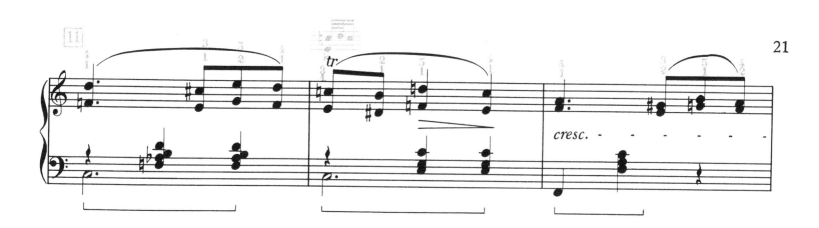

(c) This appoggiatura anticipates the 1st beat of the next measure, because it is written before the bar line. See page 11.

CANTABILE IN B♭ MAJOR

Andante moderato M.M. ♪ = 92~96

Posthumous

This work has no opus number. The autograph is signed: F.F. Chopin, Paris 1834.

POLONAISE IN B♭ MAJOR

Posthumous

Chopin composed this polonaise at the age of 7. A facsimile of the original manuscript, which was written by Chopin's father (Nicolas Chopin), was used in the preparation of this edition. The only expression mark in the manuscript is the *f* at the beginning.

The piece should be played with rhythmic vigor, and majesty, like a miniature *Polonaise Militaire*.

(a) The short appoggiatura should be played as quickly as possible, and should begin *ON THE BEAT*. See page 10.

(b) The accent is implied in the long appoggiatura. See page 10.

TRIO

Polonaise D.C. al Fine

PRELUDE IN A MAJOR

ā son ami J.C. Kessler

Op. 28, No. 7

The original autograph of the *Preludes* is in the National Library at Warsaw. Each of the preludes included in this book is edited from a microfilm of the autograph.

a The dotted wedges are added by the editor. Some pianists may consider this pedaling more acceptable on the modern piano, which has more resonance than pianos of Chopin's day.

b Students with small hands may wish to use one of the following simplifications:

MAZURKA IN G MINOR

Cantabile M.M. ♩ = 144

Op. 67, No. 2
Posthumous

No autograph of this mazurka is known to exist. The present edition is taken from the first edition of Jules Fontana, published by A.M. Schlesinger in 1855.

a The phrasing here and in the corresponding measure 54 is according to the first edition, although it is not in agreement with most modern editions, which have the following:

b Arpeggiation should be used here and in measure 54 only if the hand is too small to play all the notes of the chord simultaneously.

ⓒ The slurs in measures 33 through 40 agree with the first edition.

PRELUDE IN E MINOR
ā son ami J.C. Kessler

Op. 28, No. 4

Largo M.M. ♩ = 63~69

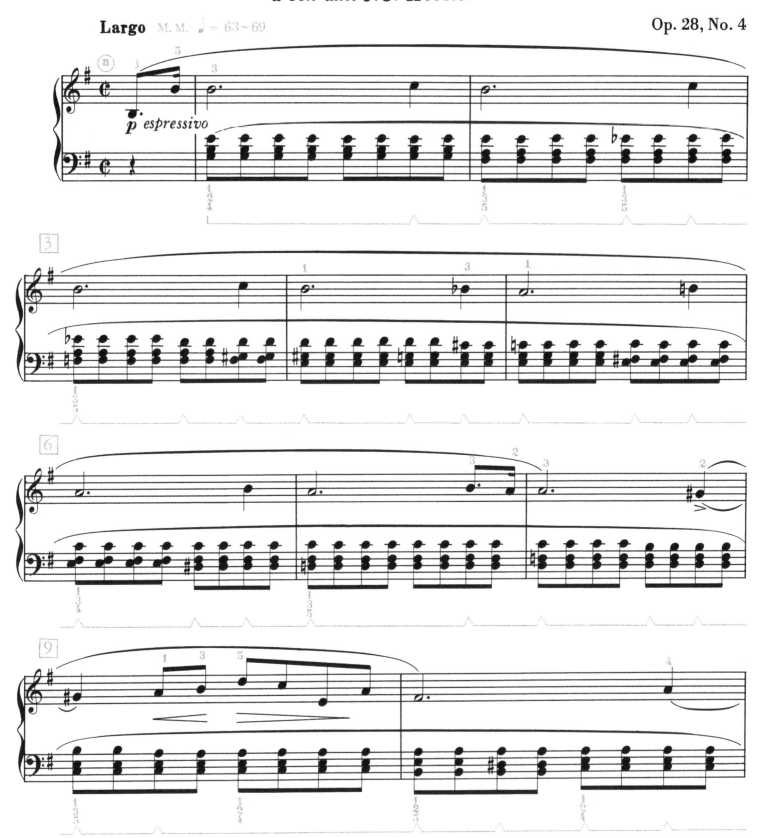

The Autograph shows no pedaling for this prelude, except in measures 17 and 18.

(a) Attention is directed to the fact that the time signature of this prelude is ¢ rather than C. It should be played with a feeling of two-in-a-bar, even though the tempo is *Largo*.

b   Many editions show a dynamic indication "p" and a diminuendo in the previous measure. The autograph has a crescendo in the 12th measure, as shown.

MAZURKA IN A MINOR

Op. 67, No. 4
Posthumous

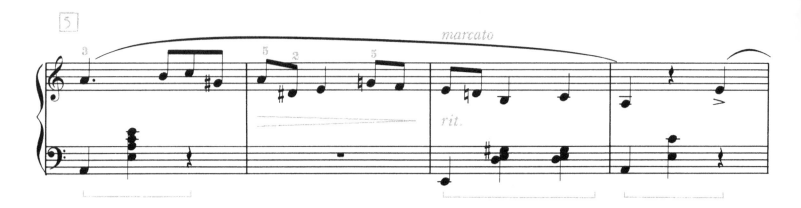

The text in dark print is based on the autograph from the estate of Johannes Brahms, now in the collection of the *Society of Friends of Music* in Vienna. Pedal indications, slurs and indications of tempo changes in light print are from first edition published by Fontana.

a   In the Fontana edition the tempo is given as *Moderato animato* ♩ = 138

b   The Fontana edition has *mf*.

c   The top note (F) in the two chords may be played with the right hand.

d   The *pp* is from a manuscript used by E. Ganche in preparation of a shorter version (Oxford Edition).

Fine

e The Oxford Edition has:

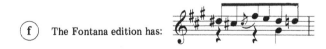

(f) The Fontana edition has:

(g) In the Fontana edition there is a crescendo beginning on the first count of measure 46, continuing to *forte* on the second count of measure 47.

LARGO IN E♭ MAJOR

Posthumous

The date of composition of this work is unknown. This edition is taken from a facsimile of the autograph published by the Chopin Institute of Warsaw. The manuscript is in the Paris Conservatoire.

MAZURKA IN F MAJOR

Op. 68, No. 3
Posthumous

Allegro, ma non troppo M. M. ♩ = 132

No autograph of this mazurka is known to exist. The present edition is taken from the first edition of Jules Fontana, published by A.M. Schlesinger in 1855.

38

Poco più vivo

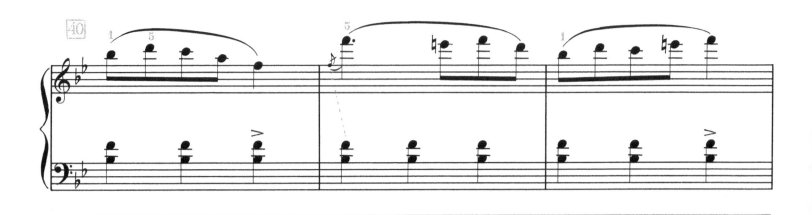

Tempo I

riten.

f

D.S. 𝄋 al Fine

POLONAISE IN G MINOR

Dédiée à son Excellence Mme. la Comtesse Victoire Skarbek

This polonaise is Chopin's first published composition. It was published in 1817, when Chopin was only seven years old. Only one copy is known to exist. It was discovered by Z. Jachemecki, who published a facsimile reprint of it in his book *F. Chopin et son oeuvre* in 1930.

The text in dark print is accurately reproduced from the reprint, except for several notes that were very obviously typographical errors. These are identified in the footnotes.

(a) The original edition has an incorrect Bb instead of C:

(b) The original edition has two incorrect F's.

(c) In the original edition the last two left hand chords are eighth notes.

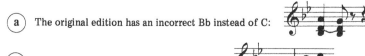

TRIO

(d) In the original edition the upper note of the left hand is a G instead of an F, an obvious error.

Polonaise D.C. al Fine

MAZURKA IN B♭ MAJOR

ā Monsieur Johns de la Nouvelle Orléans

Op. 7, No. 1

The first edition of the final version of this and the following mazurka was published by Fr. Kristner in Berlin, c. 1833. Our text in dark print accurately reproduces the first edition.

(a) All the trills in this selection may be played with more repercussions than shown in the realizations. See the discussion of this trill on page 8.

(b) This appoggiatura is discussed on page 10.

The small note should not be repeated. Its use is only to indicate that the trill begins on the principal note. The use of this small note with the trill sign seems to suggest a trill with more repercussions than the one in measure 46.

PRELUDE IN B MINOR
à son ami J.C. Kessler

Lento assai M.M. ♩ = 46~60

Op. 28, No. 6

sotto voce

The autograph shows only the pedal indications in dark print. The pedal may be applied very lightly where the indications in lighter print are shown. "Half-pedaling" may be effective here. See page 12.

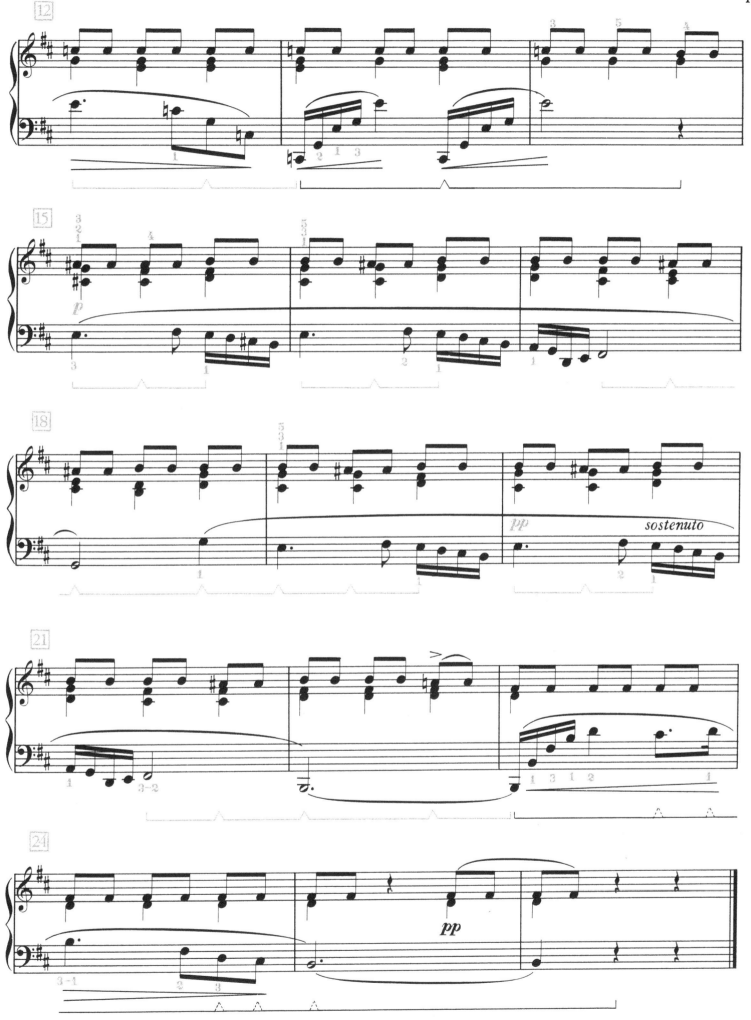

WALTZ IN A♭ MAJOR

pour M'lle. Marie Wodzińska

Tempo di Valse   M.M. ♩ = 126 ~ 132

Op. 69, No. 1
Posthumous

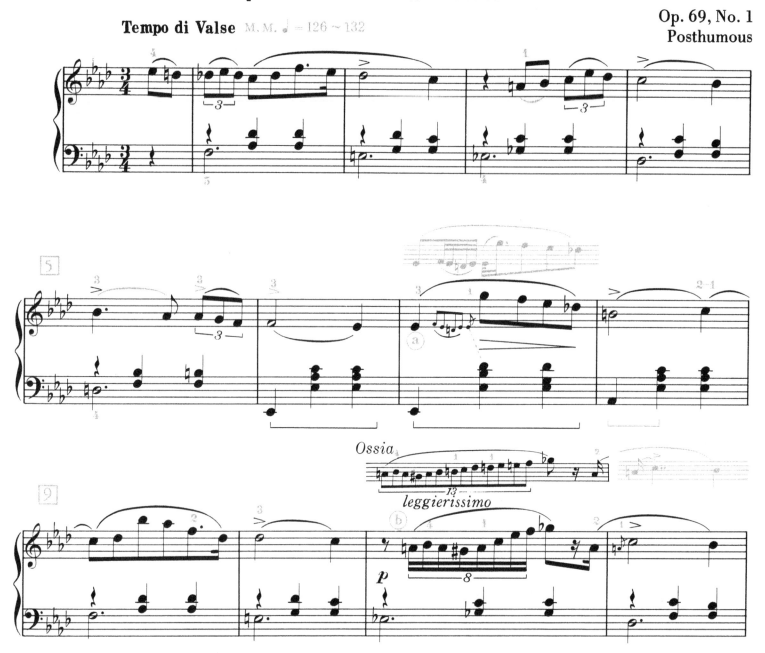

An autograph copy of this waltz was presented as a farewell gift to Marie Wodzińska, to whom Chopin was once engaged, in September of 1835. It is sometimes called *The Farewell Waltz*. The present edition faithfully reproduces this same autograph, which is now in the National Library at Warsaw. A distinctly different autograph at the Paris Conservatoire is considered to be a less refined version. The posthumous edition of Jules Fontana presents a 3rd version, not substantiated by any known autograph.

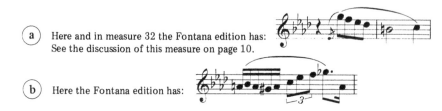

(a) Here and in measure 32 the Fontana edition has:
See the discussion of this measure on page 10.

(b) Here the Fontana edition has:

In the final appearance of this section, marked *Da Capo* in the present version, the Fontana edition has:

49

(c) In measures 13-14 and 38-39 the Fontana edition has:

(d) In the Fontana version the sixteenth rests in the right hand part in measures 18, 20 and 22 are observed only during the repeat, which is written out in full. The section is marked *con anima,* and the measures are slurred in pairs in measures 17 through 24, the first time the section is played. The left hand part is as follows:

(e) The fingering in dark print is from the autograph.

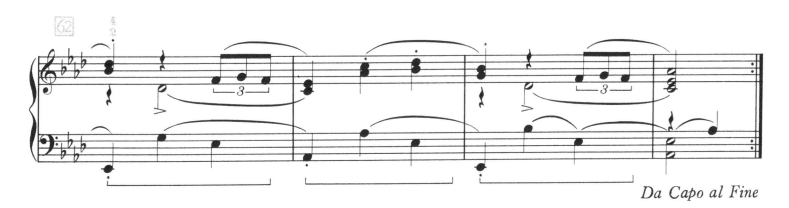

Da Capo al Fine

(d) The Fontana version has:

NOCTURNE IN C MINOR

Andante sostenuto

M.M. ♩ = 54~60

Posthumous

The date of composition of this Nocturne is unknown. This edition is taken from a facsimile of the autograph, which is now in the Paris Conservatoire.

53

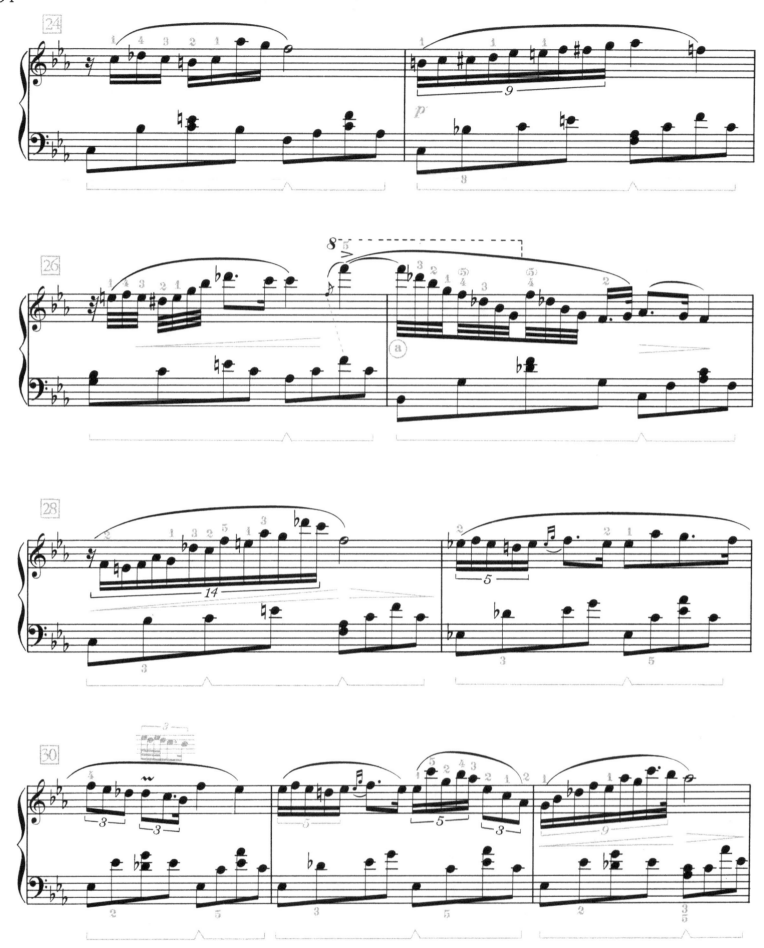

Other editions omit the G in the third group of 32nd notes in this measure, and show the remaining notes as a group of 11 16th notes. Our version is in accordance with the autograph.

POLONAISE IN A♭ MAJOR

Dédiée à Monsieur A. Żywny par Son élève Fryderyk Chopin
à Varsovie, ce 23 Avril 1821

Allegro moderato M.M. ♩ = 80~84

Posthumous

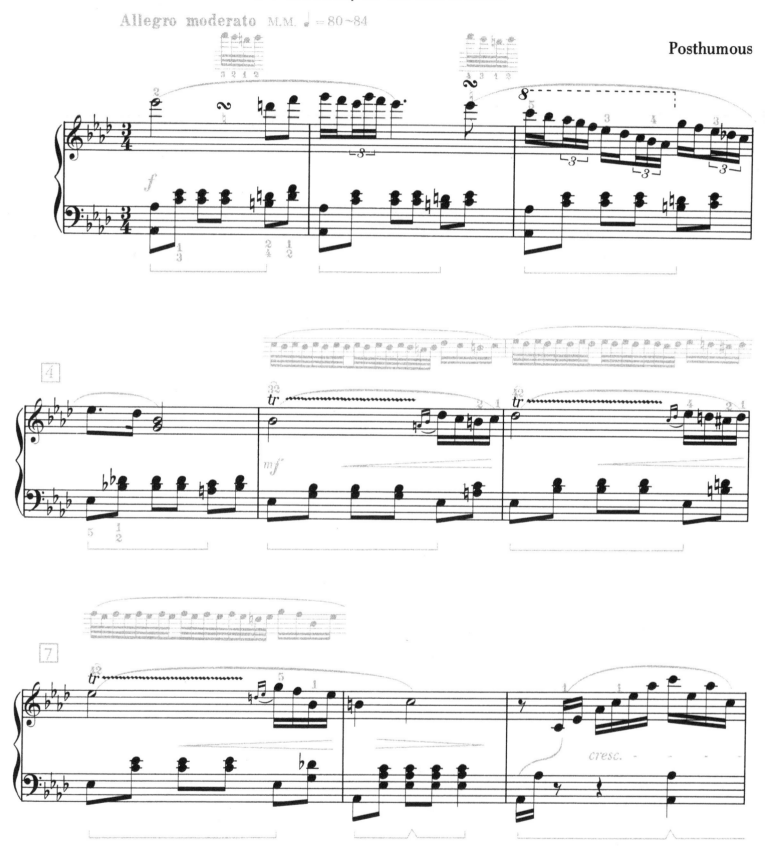

Dedicated to Monsieur A. Żywny by his pupil Frederic Chopin, at Warsaw, the 23rd of April 1821. The piece was presented to Żywny on his name-day. Chopin was 11 years old.

The autograph contains no indications of phrasing or dynamics.

(a) The trill here and in measure 38 may be played with a suffix:

b The trill here and in measure 59 may be played with a suffix:

D.C. Polonaise al Fine

WALTZ IN B MINOR

Op. 69, No. 2
Posthumous

This edition is taken from a manuscript from the Jagiellonian Library, Cracow. See the facsimile on page 3. The posthumous edition of Jules Fontana is more difficult, and not necessarily more authentic. It indicates a tempo of M.M. ♩ = 156.

(a) In the Fontana edition the repeat is written out in full, with the following differences here:

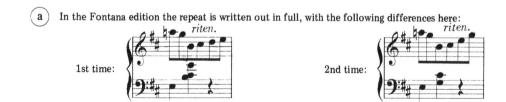

1st time: 2nd time:

b This section of the piece is to be played in a faster tempo.

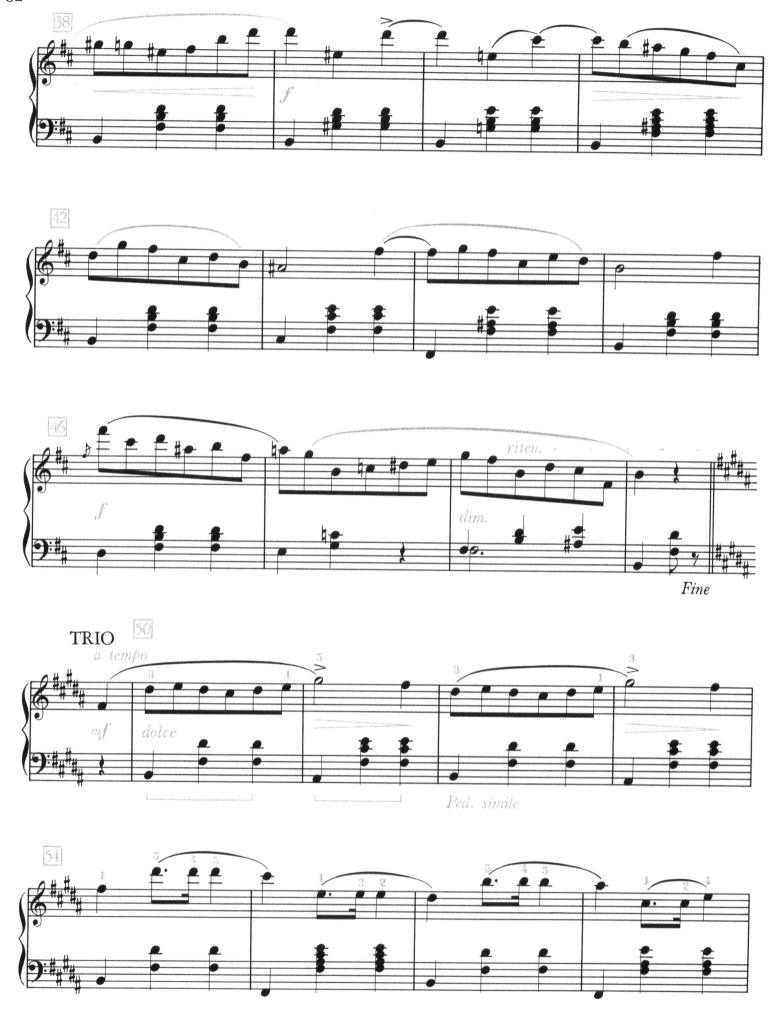

Fine

TRIO

a tempo

poco cresc.

cresc.

dim.

Waltz da Capo al Fine

(c) Most editions have:

(d) Most editions have:

PRELUDE IN C MINOR

ā son ami J.C. Kessler

Largo M.M. ♪ = 72~80

Op. 28, No. 20

(a) According to the editors of the Oxford edition, Chopin is supposed to have added a flat sign before the E in a copy belonging to one of his pupils. It does not appear in the Autograph or the original editions.

(b) *A TEMPO* is inferred by Chopin in his manner of writing these measures, which was simply to indicate that measures 5 through 8 are repeated.

(c) This is the only pedal indication in the Autograph.